To _____

From _____

THE REAL VOYAGE OF
DISCOVERY CONSISTS
NOT IN SEEKING
NEW LANDSCAPES
BUT IN HAVING
NEW EYES.

MARCEL PROUST

# Don't Look Back

Illustrated by
Mary Engelbreit

Andrews and McMeel
A Universal Press Syndicate Company
Kansas City

 is a registered trademark of
Mary Engelbreit Enterprises, Inc.

ISBN: 0-8362-1354-8

*Written by Jan Miller Girando*

# Don't Look Back

As you travel through life
there are always those times
when decisions
just have to be made ...

... when the choices are hard,
and solutions seem scarce ...

... and the rain seems
to soak your parade!

There are some situations
where all you can do
is to simply let go and move on ...

... gather courage together
and choose a direction
that carries you
toward a new dawn.

So pack up your troubles
and take a step forward—
the process of change
can be tough ...

THERE IS ALWAYS ONE MOMENT
IN CHILDHOOD WHEN THE DOOR
OPENS AND LETS THE FUTURE IN.
— GRAHAM GREENE

... but think about all
the excitement ahead
if you can be stalwart enough!

There could be adventures
you never imagined
just waiting
around the next bend ...

H A V E · A · G O O D · T R I P

... and wishes and dreams
just about to come true
in ways you can't
yet comprehend!

Perhaps you'll find friendships
that spring from new interests
as you challenge
your status quo ...

A SMALL CIRCLE OF FRIENDS

… and learn there are so many
options in life,
and so many ways you can grow!

ST. BRIGET'S
·ALL·SCHOOL·
TALENT
SHOW

MRS. PERKINS
2nd GR. as
The
SUGAR PLUM &
BEES

Perhaps you'll go places
you never expected
and see things
that you've never seen ...

... or travel to fabulous,
faraway worlds
and wonderful spots in between!

BOOKS

FALL OPEN

YOU FALL IN

ST. LOUIS PUBLIC LIBRARY

Perhaps you'll find warmth
and affection and caring—
a "somebody special"
who's there ...

... to help you stay centered
and listen with interest
to stories and feelings you share.

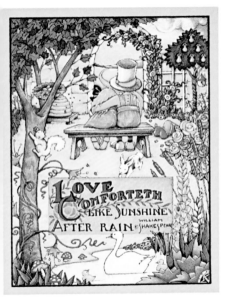

LOVE COMFORTETH LIKE SUNSHINE AFTER RAIN

WILLIAM SHAKESPEARE

Perhaps you'll find comfort
in knowing your friends are
supportive of all that you do ...

… and believe that whatever decisions you make, they'll be the right choices for you!

So keep putting one foot
in front of the other ...

... and taking your life
day by day.

There's a brighter tomorrow
that's just down the road.

Don't look back—
you're not going that way!

Always take the Scenic Route

HAVE·A·WONDERFUL·LIFE